D1759853

HONDURAS TRAVEL GUIDE FOR BEGINNERS

The Updated Concise Guide for Planning a Trip to Honduras Including Top Destinations,Culture,Outdoor Adventures,Dining,Cuisine and Getting Around

Nicolash Enzo
Copyright@2023

TABLE OF CONTENT

CHAPTER 1

INTRODUCTION

Honduras, situated in the central region of Central America, is renowned for its rich cultural legacy, captivating natural landscapes, and a historical lineage tracing back to prehistoric societies. This engaging location presents tourists with a unique amalgamation of experiences, including the exploration of ancient ruins, the immersion in bright coral reefs via diving, the engagement with local cultures, and the pursuit of exhilarating outdoor activities.

Honduras has a geographically diversified terrain, characterized by rocky mountain ranges, verdant jungles, unspoiled beaches, and lively coastal seas. Situated next to the Caribbean Sea in the north and the Pacific Ocean in the south, the nation has a coastline that spans several hundred kilometers, providing visitors with opportunities to explore a diverse range of marine marvels. The topography of the inland region of Honduras exhibits a diverse range of features, including the majestic summits of the Honduran Highlands as well as the lush lowlands characterized by a profusion of flora and fauna.

The cultural fabric of Honduras exhibits a notable level of diversity, which may be attributed to its indigenous heritage as well as the impact of European colonization. The indigenous population of the nation, including the Lenca and Maya peoples, has bequeathed a heritage characterized by cultural customs, artistic expressions, and historical import. The remnants of the ancient Maya culture may be examined at several archaeological sites, such as Copán.

At these locations, one can see finely carved stelae and pyramids, which serve as evidence of the sophisticated knowledge and artistic abilities possessed by this ancient society.

The historical importance of Honduras is further enhanced by its colonial history. The architectural structures and urban landscapes seen in locations such as Tegucigalpa, the nation's capital, provide as tangible evidence of the significant impact of Spanish influence on Honduras' metropolitan hubs. The amalgamation of cobblestone streets, colonial churches, and picturesque plazas engenders a harmonious fusion of antiquated allure and contemporary liveliness.

The northern shore is home to a thriving Garifuna population, which contributes to the cultural mix of the region. The Garifuna people make significant contributions to the cultural variety of Honduras via their own language, music, and dance forms. Individuals who visit these villages have the opportunity to engage in drumming sessions, savor authentic Garifuna cuisine, and see the vibrant art form of punta dance.

Honduras has a diverse selection of exquisite beaches that suit to the tastes of guests seeking leisure. Roatán, which is a constituent of the Bay Islands archipelago, is well recognized for its exceptionally clear seas, thriving coral reefs, and diverse array of marine fauna. Scuba divers and snorkelers are presented with a vibrant array of underwater hues when they engage in the exploration of the world's second-largest barrier reef system. In mainland Honduras, the resorts of Tela and

La Ceiba provide an ideal blend of seaside leisure and intrepid discovery, where the verdant jungles converge with the Caribbean Sea.

Honduran cuisine is characterized by a harmonious blend of indigenous tastes, colonial influences, and an abundance of seafood. Fundamental components of several Honduran culinary preparations consist of essential elements such as tortillas, beans, and rice. The baleadas, a cherished culinary creation, represent an iconic Honduran delicacy consisting of flour tortillas generously stuffed with a delectable combination of beans, cheese, and an assortment of toppings. Seafood enthusiasts will get great pleasure from savoring the most recently caught marine delicacies expertly cooked in coastal communities. Meanwhile, those in search of a gastronomic expedition may partake in the consumption of indigenous street fare such as pastelitos (deep-fried turnovers) and tajadas (fried plantains).

The nation's dedication to eco-tourism and environmental preservation is apparent in the establishment and maintenance of its national parks and protected regions. Pico Bonito National Park, exemplifying its appeal to those with a keen interest in nature, provides an array of hiking routes that meander through luxuriant woods, over resounding waterfalls, and ascend to awe-inspiring vantage spots. Cusuco National Park, renowned for its ecological significance, has a rich array of plant and animal species, including many that are unique to the local area.

Nevertheless, it is crucial for tourists to exercise caution about safety and health concerns, despite the fact that Honduras has mesmerizing natural landscapes and opportunities for personal growth. Thorough research and enough preparation are necessary while embarking on a journey, including crucial aspects such as verifying the currency of vaccines, familiarizing oneself with local traditions, and being well-informed of prevailing travel warnings.

In summary, Honduras is an intriguing place that invites more exploration. The country's rich cultural legacy, awe-inspiring natural scenery, and welcoming demeanor position it as a destination offering limitless opportunities for explorers. Honduras provides an indelible experience that is certain to create enduring memories, whether via immersing oneself in the azure seas of its coasts, exploring the enigmatic aspects of ancient civilizations, or just unwinding on its sun-drenched beaches.

CHAPTER 2

Top Destinations

Honduras, situated in Central America, is a nation renowned for its wide array of tourism sites, each possessing distinct allure, historical significance, and points of interest. Honduras offers a diverse array of tourist destinations, including busy urban centers, serene islands, historical remnants, and thriving coral reefs, therefore accommodating a broad spectrum of travel preferences. This analysis will explore many prominent places that establish Honduras as a compelling choice for those with a penchant for adventure, a keen interest in history, an affinity for beaches, and a desire to immerse themselves in other cultures.

1. Tegucigalpa: An Exploration of the Capital City

Tegucigalpa, the capital city of Honduras, presents a compelling amalgamation of historical importance and contemporary vibrancy. The city's name, which originates from the Nahuatl language, signifies silver hills, so acknowledging the historical significance of its colonial era. The historical heart of the city exhibits architectural styles from the colonial period, with notable structures such as the Metropolitan Cathedral and La Merced Church, which attract tourists due to their significant role in the city's cultural heritage. The National Art Gallery and the National Museum of Anthropology and History provide valuable perspectives on the cultural legacy of Honduras. To see expansive perspectives, individuals have the opportunity to go to El Picacho, a park situated on a hill, boasting a majestic statue of Christ and offering sweeping panoramic views of the surrounding city.

Roatán, an island located in the Caribbean Sea, is renowned for its picturesque landscapes and idyllic ambiance.

Roatán, a constituent of the Bay Islands, is an alluring Caribbean destination that entices tourists with its pristine sandy shores, crystal-clear turquoise seas, and thriving aquatic ecosystem. The island is encompassed by the Mesoamerican Barrier Reef, which is recognized as the world's second-largest barrier reef system. Consequently, it has become a highly sought-after destination for those passionate about scuba diving and snorkeling. The West End region is characterized by its vibrant assortment of restaurants, bars, and stores, contributing to a bustling atmosphere. In contrast, the West Bay Beach provides a more tranquil setting, allowing visitors to unwind under the gentle swing of palm palms. The exploration of Roatán's aquatic environment unveils a vibrant underwater ecosystem abundant with diverse coral formations, tropical marine fauna, and the potential for captivating encounters with magnificent sea turtles.

3. Copán: An Exploration of the Ancient Maya's Cultural Artifacts

The archaeological site of Copán, designated as a UNESCO World Heritage Site, has the preserved remains of a prosperous ancient Maya civilisation that flourished over an extended period of time. The archaeological site is well recognized for its highly detailed stelae, altars, and hieroglyphic stairways, which provide valuable insights into the societal aspects of the Maya upper class. The central square is prominently occupied by the Hieroglyphic Stairway, a remarkable architectural edifice embellished with hieroglyphic inscriptions that provide a comprehensive account of the historical narrative of the city. The Acropolis, including a collection of temples and monuments, serves as a tribute to the remarkable architectural accomplishments of the Maya civilization. The Copán Sculpture Museum serves to improve the whole experience by exhibiting a collection of magnificent items that have been excavated at the site.

4. Utila: Exploring the Serenity of Underwater Environments

Utila, one of the Bay Islands, has a more relaxed and cost-effective ambiance in contrast to its other islands. This location serves as an ideal destination for divers in search of a serene and unassuming environment to delve into the depths of the aquatic realm. The Caribbean Sea is home to a wide range of marine species, among them the whale shark, a majestic creature known for its kind nature. These magnificent beings are often spotted by divers exploring the region's warm waters. The island's amiable ambiance, pristine sandy coastlines, and kind residents all create an environment of serenity that is ideal for relaxation.

La Ceiba: A Portal to Exciting Experiences

La Ceiba, referred to as the Bride of Honduras, is a vibrant seaside metropolis that functions as a primary access point to many outdoor recreational activities. The close proximity of the city to Pico Bonito National Park offers individuals the chance to engage in activities such as trekking through verdant jungles, uncovering hidden waterfalls, and seeing a diverse array of avian species. The Cangrejal River provides opportunities for those seeking adventurous experiences via engaging in white-water rafting activities. On the other hand, the Cuero y Salado Wildlife Refuge extends an invitation to tourists, encouraging them to immerse themselves in the exploration of mangrove swamps and observe the diverse range of local flora and fauna. Furthermore, it is worth noting that La Ceiba is renowned for its annual Carnival festivities, which take place in May and are considered to be one of the liveliest festivals in Central America. This event showcases elaborate parades, bright music, and an array of colourful costumes.

6. Gracias: The Enduring Appeal of Colonial Charm in the Highlands

Located in the Honduran Highlands, Gracias is a captivating historical town that emanates a nostalgic atmosphere reminiscent of a bygone era. The presence of cobblestone alleys, red-tiled roofs, and well-preserved buildings effectively transports visitors to a previous historical period. The municipality serves as a starting point for the purpose of visiting Celaque National Park, an area that encompasses Cerro Las Minas, the highest summit in Honduras. The hiking routes through cloud forests, go past waterfalls, and culminate at the peak, offering expansive vistas of the surrounding regions.

These places only provide a limited overview of the options available in Honduras. Honduras has a diverse range of attractions that cater to various preferences of travelers, including the vibrant urban atmosphere of Tegucigalpa, the tranquil allure of Roatán's beaches, the ancient marvels of Copán, and the adventurous ambiance of La Ceiba and Gracias. The amalgamation of cultural legacy, natural beauty, and hospitable demeanor inside the country guarantees an indelible and remarkable expedition across its multifarious locales.

CHAPTER 3

Cultural Experiences

Honduras, a nation characterized by its abundant cultural variety and profound historical importance, presents visitors with a myriad of distinctive opportunities to explore its indigenous heritage, colonial legacy, and dynamic modern manifestations. Honduras offers tourists the opportunity to delve into its cultural history via several intriguing experiences, ranging from indulging in traditional delicacies to immersing oneself in the enchanting rhythms of local music. There are several cultural experiences that await those who go on a journey to this Central American destination.

1. Exploring the Culinary Traditions of Honduras: An Examination of Traditional Honduran Cuisine

Exploring the culinary offerings of Honduras is an essential component of a comprehensive experience in this country, as its gastronomy seamlessly combines indigenous culinary traditions, Spanish culinary influences, and locally sourced products. Fundamental components of several Honduran culinary preparations consist of essential elements such as tortillas, beans, and rice. The baleada is widely regarded as a very popular culinary creation, characterized by a folded flour tortilla that encases a delectable combination of refried beans, cheese, and an assortment of toppings like as avocado, eggs, and meat.

The plátano, also known as the plantain, assumes a prominent role in several culinary preparations, such as tajadas, which are slices of plantain that are fried, and maduros, which are sweet fried plantains.

Seafood has a prominent position within coastal areas, whereby the use of freshly caught marine resources results in the creation of delectable ceviches and stews infused with coconut. The Honduran dish often referred to as sopa de caracol, which translates to conch soup in English, is renowned for its rich tastes and the communal dining practice associated with it. Individuals with a penchant for culinary exploration may also consider sampling chicharrones de cerdo, which are delectably crispy hog skins that are often accompanied by yuca and pickled onions.

2. Investigating Regional Markets and Artisanal Crafts

The markets in Honduras are dynamic centers of commerce, where residents convene for the purposes of purchasing goods, engaging in social interactions, and exhibiting their creative talents. Traversing these bustling marketplaces is a multisensory experience, as the olfactory allure of street cuisine intermingles with the vivid hues of fabrics and handicrafts. The Mercado Guamilito located in San Pedro Sula and the Mercado San Isidro situated in Tegucigalpa are well recognized marketplaces known for their diverse range of products, including fresh agricultural food as well as intricately manufactured souvenirs.

Honduras has a diverse array of handicrafts, including elaborate woodcarvings, vivid fabrics, and intricately woven baskets. La Esperanza, a municipality situated in the elevated region of the Honduran Highlands, has gained recognition for its exceptional craftsmanship in the production of Lenca pottery. This distinctive kind of pottery is distinguished by its striking geometric patterns and a color palette that mostly features earthy tones. By engaging in the exploration of these marketplaces, tourists are given the opportunity to not only acquire genuine mementos, but also get valuable knowledge on the intergenerational transmission of craftsmanship.

3. Exploring the Cultural Significance of Music and Dance

Music and dance play a significant role in the cultural fabric of Honduras, providing a valuable insight into the profound emotions and essence of its populace. The Garifuna population, which is mostly located along the northern coast of the nation, makes a substantial contribution to the musical landscape of the region. The rhythmic and colorful drumming of the Garifuna community, together with their traditional dance forms such as punta, effectively embody the essence of their African and Caribbean cultural lineage. Travel enthusiasts have the opportunity to engage in drumming courses, dancing classes, and cultural events as means of achieving a comprehensive immersion in this vibrant artistic expression.

In addition to the distinctive Garifuna rhythms, Honduras showcases a diverse array of music genres that exemplify the country's rich ethnic heritage. The musical genre known as Parranda is often performed at celebratory events, including the prominent use of guitars, maracas, and expressive lyrics. The marimba, a traditional instrument resembling a xylophone, is a prominent feature in Honduran music, generating melodic compositions that elicit feelings of nostalgia and festivity.

4. The Preservation of Garifuna Culture: Safeguarding Traditional Practices

The Garifuna people have a distinctive position within the cultural fabric of Honduras. The historical background of this region exhibits a confluence of indigenous Carib, African, and Arawak elements, which emerged via a process of cultural amalgamation that transpired many centuries in the past. Individuals who go on journeys to Garifuna villages, such as Livingston and Triunfo de la Cruz, have the opportunity to see the preservation of longstanding cultural practices. These communities often provide a warm welcome to guests, providing them with valuable knowledge about their cultural practices, gastronomic traditions, and creative manifestations.

Engaging in a customary dugu ritual, characterized by musical performances, dance, and the presentation of gifts to ancestral figures, provides an opportunity to gain insight into the spiritual convictions that form the foundation of Garifuna cultural practices. By actively participating in storytelling sessions, drumming performances, and shared meals, individuals may get a more profound understanding of the resilience and vibrancy shown by this distinctive cultural community.

5. Festival Celebrations: Participation in Festive Gatherings

Festivals have significant importance in the Honduran society as they serve as integral platforms for communal gatherings, festivities, and the preservation of cultural heritage. Semana Santa, often known as Holy Week, is a very important religious observance characterized by processions, intricate street carpets, and customary reenactments depicting the Passion of Christ. The Semana Santa festivities are widely followed across the nation, with notable recognition given to Antigua, Copán, and Comayagua for their famed celebrations.

The annual Carnival in La Ceiba is a dynamic and energetic event that serves as a platform for showcasing the city's exuberant character. The streets are enlivened with parades, street parties, and music performances, ultimately ending in the crowning of a Carnival queen. The festive atmosphere and enthusiastic display of emotions throughout the event provide a riveting glimpse into the exuberant characteristics inherent in Honduran cultural traditions.

Honduras may be described as a complex amalgamation of indigenous cultural heritage, colonial historical influences, and modern-day manifestations. By means of its culinary traditions, artisanal products, musical expressions, dance forms, and celebratory events, individuals embarking on journeys are afforded the chance to actively participate in and establish meaningful connections with the dynamic cultural fabric of a particular locale, beyond geographical boundaries. As one traverses the many cultural encounters inside the nation, it becomes evident that the authentic nature of Honduras is encapsulated in the narratives, musical cadences, and customary practices that contribute to its distinctiveness.

CHAPTER 4

Outdoor Adventures

Honduras, characterized by its varied topography including verdant rainforests and unspoiled coastlines, is an appealing destination for those with a penchant for outdoor pursuits, offering exhilarating experiences and opportunities for intimate engagement with the natural environment. Honduras has a diverse range of outdoor experiences suitable for those with varying degrees of interest in adventure, including activities such as traversing challenging terrains and exploring the depths of the Caribbean Sea.

Let us explore a selection of thrilling outdoor activities that await those who embark on a journey to this captivating destination in Central America.

1. National Parks and Wildlife Reserves: An Exploration of Nature's Richness

Honduras has a comprehensive system of national parks and wildlife reserves, which allow individuals the chance to engage in immersive experiences with its abundant biodiversity. Pico Bonito National Park, also referred to as the Emerald Forest, is a highly sought-after location among enthusiasts of natural environments. The rainforests in this region possess a high level of biodiversity, hosting a wide variety of plant and animal species, including as jaguars, howler monkeys, and diverse avian populations. The hiking routes provide access to concealed waterfalls, unspoiled pools, and awe-inspiring views that provide expansive panoramas of the surrounding terrain.

Cusuco National Park, located inside the Honduran Highlands, is a notable destination that appeals to those seeking eco-adventures. The cloud woods inside the park provide a habitat for a variety of rare orchids, elusive quetzals, and several kinds of amphibians. The guided treks conducted in this beautiful landscape provide valuable insights into the significance of conservation efforts and the intricate equilibrium of the ecosystem.

2. Hiking and Trekking Adventures: Overcoming Mountain Peaks and Wilderness Trails

The diverse geography of Honduras offers a range of chances for those with varying degrees of hiking and trekking experience. Ascending Cerro Las Minas in Celaque National Park is regarded as a walk that presents both formidable difficulties and gratifying experiences. Being the highest point in Honduras, this mountain provides explorers with the opportunity to successfully ascend its top, so giving them panoramic views of cloud forests, valleys, and neighboring mountains.

The Cangrejal River Valley, located near La Ceiba, has a variety of paths that traverse verdant forests and meander beside pristine rivers, catering to those seeking a less strenuous trekking experience. The El Bejuco Waterfall Trail offers access to a visually striking waterfall, providing travelers with the opportunity to engage in a revitalizing swim inside the naturally formed pool located underneath it.

3. Aquatic Sports and Adventurous Pursuits: Embracing the Elements of Water and Challenging Rapids

The coastal region of Honduras is characterized by the presence of picturesque beaches and abundant marine biodiversity in its coastal waters. Roatán, a globally recognized scuba diving location, attracts enthusiasts of underwater exploration due to its thriving coral reefs and diverse array of marine animals. Snorkelers and divers have the opportunity to engage in close proximity with reef sharks, sea turtles, and a diverse array of vibrant fish species, therefore experiencing an immersive encounter inside an enchanting aquatic environment.

The Cangrejal River is an opportunity for anyone in search of a heightened sense of excitement to engage in spectacular white-water rafting activities. The river's composition, consisting of alternating sections of strong currents and tranquil portions, renders it well-suited for those of varying levels of expertise in the sport of rafting. While traversing the rapids, individuals will find themselves immersed in the awe-inspiring splendor of the rainforest, resulting in an experience that seamlessly combines exhilaration and tranquility.

4. Canopy Tours and Ziplining: An Exploration of Aerial Adventure in Natural Environments

The lush jungles of Honduras provide an ideal environment for engaging in canopy tours and ziplining excursions. The Cangrejal River Valley provides ziplining opportunities that enable anyone to traverse the uppermost levels of the forest, giving them the chance to see rare avian species and verdant vegetation while swiftly moving between designated stations. This distinctive viewpoint offers an aerial vantage point of the dynamic ecology situated underneath.

The Sambo Creek region in La Ceiba provides canopy excursions that include ziplining and aerial bridges, allowing individuals to go through the forest canopy and see its diverse ecosystems in close proximity. These expeditions not only provide an exhilarating surge of adrenaline but also foster a more profound affinity with the natural environment.

5. The Intersection of Eco-Tourism and Conservation: Establishing a Connection with the Natural Environment

The dedication of Honduras to eco-tourism and conservation initiatives is apparent via the many options it provides for guests to actively participate in nature-related activities while simultaneously supporting its preservation. The Whale Shark Research and Conservation Project in Utila offers an opportunity for guests to engage in snorkeling excursions, enabling them to see the presence of these docile creatures while actively supporting continuous research efforts and conservation activities.

Moreover, the eco-lodges and sustainable hotels in Honduras provide an opportunity for guests to deeply engage with the natural environment while simultaneously reducing their ecological footprint. The decision to stay in these lodges not only provides a unique and deeply engaging encounter, but also contributes to the development of local communities and the preservation of natural resources.

In summary, Honduras presents itself as an ideal destination for those who like outdoor activities and seek adventure, providing a wide range of possibilities to engage with the natural environment, push personal boundaries, and experience the excitement of outdoor pursuits. Honduras has a range of various landscapes that provide visitors with remarkable experiences, fostering a heightened sense of admiration for the natural world. These experiences may include trekking through misty cloud forests, immersing oneself in the pristine waters of the Caribbean, or traversing the treetops through a zipline.

CHAPTER 5

Honduran cuisine

Honduran cuisine is characterized by the harmonious amalgamation of native products, Spanish culinary traditions, and Caribbean taste profiles, resulting in a multifaceted gastronomic fabric that aptly represents the nation's cultural legacy and geographical variations. Honduran cuisine has a diverse range of culinary offerings that include both traditional savory meals and colorful street food, providing a rich exploration of historical and gastronomic elements. This analysis aims to examine the complexities of Honduran cuisine, including its constituent materials, culinary creations, and the cultural implications that contribute to its exceptional nature as a gastronomic encounter.

Ingredients: A Plethora of Flavors

The nation of Honduras benefits from its fertile terrain and diversified ecosystems, which contribute to a rich assortment of ingredients that serve as the fundamental building blocks of its culinary traditions. Corn, beans, and rice are fundamental ingredients in several culinary preparations, symbolizing the rich indigenous legacy of the nation. Corn is used in the preparation of tortillas, tamales, and several other customary culinary preparations, whilst beans are often served alongside meals, offering a valuable source of protein and nutritional content.

Tropical fruits, such as mangoes, pineapples, and papayas, provide a vibrant infusion of taste and visual appeal to a diverse range of culinary preparations, including both savory and sweet compositions. The coconut, a widely used component in culinary practices throughout coastal regions, is often incorporated into a variety of dishes including curries, sweets, and beverages. Plantains, which are closely related to bananas, have a remarkable versatility as a culinary component, capable of being subjected to frying, boiling, or mashing techniques to provide a diverse array of gastronomic creations.

Traditional Cuisine: Exploring Culinary Heritage

Baleadas are a traditional Honduran dish that consists of a flour tortilla filled with various ingredients such as refried beans, The baleada, a renowned culinary creation originating from Honduras, is characterized by a folded flour tortilla that encases a delectable combination of refried beans, cheese, and an assortment of toppings.

This simple but gratifying culinary creation is a fundamental component of both street gastronomy and domestic cuisine, offering a prompt and savory repast.

2. Archetypal Plato: Denoting the typical plate, this culinary creation epitomizes the essence of Honduran gastronomy. The customary composition of this dish often comprises of rice, beans, a protein source (such as chicken, beef, or hog), fried plantains, and sometimes a basic salad. The amalgamation of these constituents epitomizes the gastronomic customs of the nation inside a unified and substantial repast.

The topic of discussion is Sopa de Caracol. The conch soup is a highly esteemed cultural delicacy, known for its substantial and satisfying qualities. Enriched with coconut milk, an assortment of veggies, and a blend of spices, this culinary creation provides a sensory encounter that is both indulgent and fragrant. Sopa de caracol, when accompanied by a serving of rice or tortillas, exemplifies the profound impact of Caribbean tastes on the culinary traditions of Honduras.

One popular dish in Latin American cuisine is Yuca con Chicharrón. The yuca, a tuberous vegetable with a high starch content, undergoes a process of boiling until it reaches a state of tenderness, followed by frying to provide a desirable crispy texture on the outer surface. It is often served with chicharrón, which refers to hog skins that have been deep-fried to get a crispy texture. The amalgamation of diverse textures and tastes renders a highly sought-after culinary choice within the realm of street cuisine.

One popular dish in Latin American cuisine is Sopa de Mondongo. This robust soup made with tripe exemplifies the impact of Spanish culinary traditions on Honduran gastronomy. Sopa de mondongo, a popular dish among locals, is prepared with tripe, veggies, and a variety of spices. This comforting culinary creation is often accompanied by tortillas.

Title: Cultural Significance: Exploring the Culinary Heritage Introduction: The cultural significance of culinary traditions is an important aspect of heritage preservation. This essay aims to delve into the importance of culinary practices as a means to preserve and celebrate cultural heritage. By examining the role of food in shaping

The culinary traditions of Honduras are a reflection of the nation's historical development and its rich cultural variety. The convergence of indigenous traditions, Spanish colonial influences, and African ancestry results in a cohesive amalgamation of diverse tastes and culinary methods. Culinary traditions often exhibit a strong interconnection with religious festivities and familial assemblies, so accentuating their cultural importance.

In Honduras, meals often exhibit a communal nature, when individuals gather with their relatives and friends to partake in shared sustenance, engage in storytelling, and express joviality. The use of conventional culinary techniques, shown by the employment of clay comals in the production of tortillas, serves as a means of establishing a cultural link between contemporary Hondurans and their predecessors, so preserving and perpetuating their ancestral customs and traditions.

Street food and local markets play a crucial role in the daily lives of people.

The street food culture and local markets in Honduras provide an immersive opportunity to explore the country's everyday life and culinary heritage. Mercado Guamilito, located in San Pedro Sula, and Mercado San Isidro, situated in Tegucigalpa, are two vibrant marketplaces renowned for their diverse array of street food offerings. Visitors to these busy markets may indulge in a wide range of culinary delicacies, ranging from freshly prepared baleadas to delectable sweet pastries.

Eco-tourism and culinary experiences have become more popular, with a particular focus on farm-to-table adventures.

In line with the global adoption of sustainable practices, Honduras is actively engaging in the development of eco-tourism initiatives and promoting farm-to-table experiences. Travel enthusiasts have the opportunity to deeply engage with the gastronomic realm by embarking on visits to indigenous farms and actively participating in customary culinary instructional sessions. These experiences provide valuable insights on the procurement of goods and the traditional

culinary methods used in Honduran
kitchens.

In summary, Honduran cuisine embodies
the intricate tapestry of its extensive
historical background, diverse cultural
heritage, and plentiful natural endowments.
Each component conveys a narrative,
ranging from the earthy notes of maize and
beans to the tropical richness of fruits and
coconut. Traditional culinary preparations
have the ability to foster a sense of unity
and cohesion among communities, as they
serve as a common ground for individuals
to gather and connect. Conversely, street
food encapsulates the essence of everyday
existence, reflecting the vibrant and
dynamic nature of daily living. As one
indulges in the many tastes of Honduran
cuisine, an exploration ensues, including
historical narratives, cultural nuances, and

the communal delight derived from the act of dining together.

THE END